NEW SPECIES, NEW RACE OF HUMAN BEINGS

NEW SPECIES, NEW RACE OF HUMAN BEINGS

Bishop Prientiss Thomas

fruitful.poetic.light

Copyright © 2020 Prientiss Thomas

St. Louis, Missouri
ISBN: 9798636002925
Publisher: fruitful.poetic.light
All rights reserved

All scripture quotations, unless otherwise indicated, are taken from the Holy Bible, King James Version® KJV® Copyright © King James Version, Thomas Nelson Publisher, Nashville, Tennessee, 1989. Used by permission. Scripture quotations taken from the Amplified Bible are used by permission.

No part of this book may be reproduced or transmitted in any form or by any means, electronic or mechanical—including photocopy, recording, or by any information storage and retrieval system—without permission in writing from the publisher. Please direct your inquires to: prophetprientiss@gmail.com

Printed in the United States of America

CONTENTS

New species, new race of human beings
Title Page
Copyright
Introduction
CHRIST IN YOU THE HOPE OF GLORY   1
UNDERSTANDING THE INNER MAN   5
MY ASSIGNMENT   7
THE NEW SPECIES   9
SEED PRODUCTION   13
GOD AT WORK IN THE NEW SPECIES   17
FUNCTION LIKE GOD   19
PRODUCTS OF THE RESURRECTION   23
NO LONGER COMMON   27
A SUPERIOR RACE OF BEINGS   31
OPERATING FAITH FROM A DIFFERENT POSITION   35
THE ZOE LIFE OF GOD   41
WHAT IS DEATH?   43
NEW SPECIES DAILY CONFESSION   53
BIBLIOGRAPHY   57

INTRODUCTION

In the year 2001, while I was relaxing and reflecting in a hotel not far from our house in West County, Missouri, I heard the audible voice of the Lord. I wasn't alone, for one of the armor-bearers that I was training was with me. This time it was my nephew Bro. Claynon. He not only had to perform servant duties to me, but my wife (his aunt) and I were also sending him through college at the same time. So many times, he had to do his school work and serve the Pastor at the same time.

Well, this particular day he was with me and had just left to go to school that morning from the hotel. After he left, I went into my routine of prayer and worship! This time, I started with several Scriptures on repentance and cleanings because I learned to confess also the sins of the people (the congregation) before the Lord. As I stood before the Lord to read this particular series of Scriptures (I was reading from Psalm 51), about mid-way within the verses I was reading, all of a sudden I heard this audible voice. Now this voice did not come from within me for I would have recognized it because I have experienced this many times, but this voice was outside of me, and I must add that I have experienced this also before.

While standing there, the voice said, "YOU ARE ONE WITH ME!" As soon as I heard it, while standing there with the Bible in both of my hands, I hollered out loudly,

"OOOHHH!" And the Bible went one way and I fell across the bed! I was breathing very hard and my heart was racing! And I am still saying Oh! Oh! Oh! And in my mind, I immediately started trying to figure out what just happened and at the same time, I'm saying, "Yes Lord, yes Lord." That's all I knew to say! I was frightened, yet calm; I was curious, yet delighted; I was at a loss for words, yet excited!

Finally, I sat up and I'm wondering what just happened, and I did say, "Who are you Lord?" Quickly in my mind, theologically speaking, I knew it couldn't have been an angel because we cannot be one with angels, and so I'm wondering who you are. Mind you all this is going on in my head, and I'm saying was this Jesus or was this God because it sounded like a man's voice; not an earthquake kind of voice with the rocks breaking and the thunder and lighting and the wind blowing in a very dramatic type of scenario, but it was real! Super real! Oh! I do want to say that I didn't feel anything before the voice spoke audibly, and I didn't feel anything afterward either. Of course, you know that was the end of that prayer and confessing time.

I wrote it down in my journal notes and meditated upon it. Why would He say this to me? I didn't feel like this was something that he should be saying to me. Although I am a Pastor and a prophet of God, I do fast, pray, and spend numerous hours in prayer unto God, yet I still have so much work that needs to be done on me and in me. Why would He say that to me: "YOU ARE ONE WITH ME?" What is He saying, and again why is He saying it to me? It didn't make me feel powerful at that time and "all that." It actually made me humble myself even the more and search my heart, and at the same time I wanted to hear and receive whatever it is that He was saying and whatever it is that He wants me to do with this.

It sort of reminds me of John the Baptist being told by Father God that he would see the Holy Spirit descend upon the one who is the Messiah and he was to baptize him and to say, "Behold the lamb of God which takes away the sins of the world!" My God, John, when he saw Jesus, he said, "I'm not worthy even to untie your shoes," but he was born for that purpose: to **forerun** the first coming of Jesus. Maybe he wasn't worthy—who is? But God chose him, and regardless of how he dressed, what he looked like, what he smelled like etc., he was God's choice.

I told everyone at the church and at home what happened. Now this was not the first time that I had an encounter with God that was very supernatural!

Then about two weeks later, while at home in my study praying and worshiping God, actually I was in fellowship with "The Blessed Holy Spirit" while sitting in my chair, and for some reason, my mind went back to what happened that morning in the hotel. Immediately after that thought passed through my mind, I so happened to reach down to pick up some materials off of the floor, and as soon as I reached down to pick up the papers off of the floor, the Lord spoke to me in a flash (now this voice was inside of me, not outside me) and said, "THE SAME THAT SAID LET US MAKE MAN IN OUR IMAGE AND AFTER OUR LIKENESS!" I gasped and said, "OH my God! That was ELOHIM speaking to ME in that hotel room that morning." What a relief! God is so faithful. Now everything was so clear!

In St. John 17:21-23, Jesus is talking to Father God about our oneness with Him and with the Father. This is a very important piece in our total redemptive package: oneness. Why am I saying this? I am saying this because I have seen Elohim (God) before this visitation happened, and I had been studying Scriptures about Him, and receiving revelation about His activity in the Word of God and his dealings with the people of God. Well, you can read about my visitation and revelatory encounter with him in my book, <u>Elohim the Order of Mankind Creation.</u>

There are two parts to being created in the image and likeness of God. The first is all human beings are created in the image and likeness of God by order of our creation. There are multiple Scriptures to that fact; for instance, Acts 17: 24-27. However, this image of God through procreation cannot give or impart eternal life to anyone. Why? Because of the fall of man, everyone born of Adam has the sin nature in them. The second is we must become the image of God through Christ Jesus, meaning we must repent and be born again. Now this second image of God is the one that we are focusing on in this teaching.

CHRIST IN YOU THE HOPE OF GLORY

After that experience with the audible voice, I found myself studying and focusing on the phrase "Christ in you the hope of glory." That's how the Scripture put it in Colossians 1:27, **"to whom God was pleased to make known what is the riches of the glory of this mystery among the Gentiles, which is Christ in you, the hope of glory."**

However, I found myself saying it this way: "CHRIST IN ME MANIFESTING HIS HOPE OF GLORY THROUGH ME IN THE EARTH REALM." Let's take a look at another Scripture:

> *I bow my knees unto the Father of our Lord Jesus Christ, of whom the whole family in heaven and earth is named, (Ephesians 3:14-15).*

In addition to the above description of what we are in Christ Jesus, the believer is called *"righteousness"* and the unbeliever is called *"unrighteousness."* The believer is called *"light"* and the unbeliever is called *"darkness."*

Second Corinthians 6:14 states, **"Be ye not unequally yoked together with unbelievers: for what fellowship hath righteousness with unrighteousness? And what communion hath light with darkness?"**

Finally, the believer is called *"Christ"* and the unbeliever is called *"Belial."* Second Corinthians 6:15 states, **"... and what concord hath Christ with Belial?"**

Jesus is the Head of the Body of Christ and we are the members of that body. You don't call your head by one name and your arms and legs by another name because all parts of you (big or small) make up one body. In this passage, Paul calls the individual members of the Body of Christ, "Christ" and he calls the unbeliever, "Belial".

Listen, Christ is in you right now and that puts the hope of glory in you. First Corinthians 3:15 states, **"Know ye not that ye are the temple of God and that the Spirit of God dwelleth in you?"** You've got God the Father, God the Son, and God the Holy Spirit living in you.

Romans 8:10-11 states, **"... and if Christ is in you, the body is dead because of sin, but the Spirit is life because of righteousness. But if the Spirit of Him who raised Jesus from the dead dwells in you, He who raised Christ from the dead will also give life to your mortal bodies through His Spirit who dwells in you."**

The Scriptures tell about two types of deaths mankind experiences because of the fall of Adam: natural and spiritual. Natural death is the separation of the spirit-soul from the physical body. Spiritual death is eternal separation from the presence of God. Those in Christ Jesus were once alienated from God—dead in trespasses, but because of faith in the sacrifice Jesus made, believers are now spiritually alive and will spend eternity in God's presence. YOU WILL NEVER DIE AGAIN! SO, DO NOT BE AFRAID OF DEATH.

We've never even majored on these great Bible truths. These truths will release us, make us masters, and enable us to dominate and reign in life. The NEW man is Christ in you; a son has been born in you or recreated in you. God recreated Christ in you—a son. And now at this end-time all of creation is waiting on what's inside of you to come forth, hallelujah!

This led to my quest to find out what the image of God is as it pertains to the inner man: the **YOU** inside of this flesh house—and that **YOU** inside of this flesh house is a **NEW** species: a new race of beings. I wanted to know what this new race was all about; what can it do, and how does it operate.

Over and over again in my prayer and fellowship time with God, He would talk with me about who we are and what we are and how we are to operate. He would tell me and challenge me to ACT like God is my Father just like He is Jesus' Father. Because I have his nature now, that old nature is gone! My human spirit is recreated in the image of God through Christ Jesus, and it has the nature of God in it, which is mind blowing in and of itself.

I had questions as to why we haven't really majored in that part of us in the churches! I started to explode with revelation; such as, "If I have the nature of God in me then I must be like Him on the inside of me and what does that mean, what can it do? Why is it important to do so now? What would happen if people really learned about it and how it functions—what it can really do? Wow! The main point is this: JESUS MADE THE NEW SPECIES A REALITY FOR ALL OF US! So, let's dig into some pretty neat information and revelation about what we are: New Species, New Race. Let's put this *new species, new race* to work for God's glory. Amen!

UNDERSTANDING THE INNER MAN

When the Scripture declares that "if any man be in Christ he is a new creature," it is talking about the new creature in your **inner man.** Remember, in fulfillment of what was prophesied through the prophet Ezekiel, man receives a **new nature** at the **new birth** experience. God has placed His very **nature** in the **spirit** of those who experience the new birth.

> *A new heart also will I give you, and a new spirit will I put within you: and I will take away the Stony heart out of your flesh, and I will give you a heart of flesh. And I will put my spirit within you, and cause you to walk in my statues, and ye shall keep my judgments, and do them (Ezekiel 36:26-27).*

The word *HEART* (Hebrew: Labe) refers to the center of man's affections. The word SPIRIT (Hebrew: Ruach) refers to "by resemblance breath or spirit of a rational being including its expression and functions." **For anyone who is in Christ Jesus, the sinful nature that was against God is gone.** The sinful nature has been replaced with God's very own nature. The Scripture states, *"Therefore if any person is [engrafted] in Christ (the Messiah) he is a new creation (a new creature altogether); the old [previous moral and spir-*

itual condition] has passed away..." (2 Corinthians 5:17 Amplified).

Looking to that **new nature** means to speak from the revelation of what it is and to exercise your faith through the knowledge that it is the **nature of God** in you. Plus, when you accept what the word says about you and what you can do with the reality of who you are, you know and understand that if you have the **nature of God** in you, then you have the ability of God in your **inner man**. Now you are identifying with it and therefore allowing it to come alive in you and manifest through you. When you act like you have the nature of God in your **inner man** that changes everything. Hallelujah! These are some of the principles of looking to the new **inner man;** it changes your view of yourself and increases your faith's operational ability.

MY ASSIGNMENT

<u>**The making and manifesting of the sons of God with power for end-time purposes is my assignment and purpose.**</u> For all of creation is waiting on the sons of God to manifest!

Believers are "A New Species of Being:" a new man created by God through Christ Jesus to rule and reign with Him in this life (Rom. 5:17). A new breed of human beings who have the life of God in them, that will never spiritually die, and who have immortality in them right now—not when they go to heaven. Believers are a new species that can talk and communicate with the Father, God the Son, God the Holy Spirit, angels, demons, and other beings in dominions and places. Believers are a new creation that can travel to other places by the Holy Spirit.

The new species can walk with God and operate like Him —and be in his presence without fear and intimidation. The new creation, this new species, is just like God: imperishable and eternal. This new species has power and ability from God within it. As a matter of fact, the new species has the ability of God in it right now. This new species, a new race of beings, can exercise faith like it's Father God, for this new species is a superhuman race because of its godlike nature. This new race is to act just like Christ in the earth realm, and the more your mind is renewed to your real identity, no situation or circumstance will be able to stand in your way! Everything that God has is made available to the new species.

What God started in Genesis 1:26 continues to work in this new species of being. We must understand how faith in Jesus has reversed the fall and produced a new species of being. Second Corinthians 5:17 from the Amplified Bible states, **"Therefore if any person is [engrafted] in Christ (the Messiah) he is a new creation (a new creature altogether); the old [previous moral and spiritual condition] have passed away. Behold the fresh and new has come!"** Believers are A NEW SPECIES OF BEING THAT NEVER BEFORE EXISTED!

The new species is not under Satan's dominion or control. The Scriptures tell us in 1 John 5:4 that **"whatsoever is born of God overcometh the world…"** Expect answers to your prayers. As a matter of fact, knowing who you are in Christ Jesus helps your prayer life and ability to receive because your prayers go up drastically to a higher frequency!

We are one with him through the new birth—the new species is one with God! The new species can master demons and situations greater now, and no weapon formed against that image shall prosper (Isaiah 54:17). What does this mean? It means that the new species shall prosper! Bullets and guns can only release you from this flesh house, but they cannot destroy your spirit-soul because you are immortal and you have immortality like God your Father (St. Matt. 10:28). Jesus came that we might have this new life and that more abundantly (St. John 10:10). Divine intellect is available for you to know the thoughts of God by the Holy Spirit (1 Corinthians 2:10, 12).

THE NEW SPECIES

The phrase, *new species*, means: New breed of—a new type of - a new entity, a new brand. This means that you are a particular race of beings from the human race of beings that God created. We are called "the human race," but the born-again person has experienced the new birth through repentance, regeneration by the word, and the Spirit of God has brought them into the kingdom of God and produced a new species of being. This new race of human beings is now superior to the ordinary human beings (those not born again--unbelievers) because the new race (believers) have the life God in them. To tell you the truth, you are now one with God through the new birth experience, but we have never majored on it in the church; that is, your oneness with God. You are now one with God because you have His nature in your spirit, and you have his Holy Spirit abiding in you. This oneness with God is designed to change your thinking and believing in the way you live your life (your lifestyle), and in the way you operate in this life (your interaction with others).

You are now a superior being not in a "nose-stuck-in-the-air" type of thing, for that is not the spirit character and personality of Jesus. The superior being that you are is an extraordinary life and you will live an extraordinary life as you operate in who you are, what you are, and how you are learning to operate your faith according to your identity.

Having been created in the likeness of God, the likeness of God in you touches other people, and the likeness of God in you is transferable. By transferring the peace of God in you to others, this life of God in you can be shared. The reason why you can act like this, the reason why you can speak like this, and the reason why you can make demands like this is because you are a new species, a new race, and you should expect results because of it. If I am speaking to things, conditions, and the devil from the knowledge and understanding of who I am in Christ, what do you think the results will be?

According to the dictionary, **new creation** means, "the action or process of bringing something into existence." The word, **species** means, "*A group of living organisms consisting of similar individuals capable of exchanging genes or interbreeding.* The species is the principal natural taxonomic unit, ranking below a genus and denoted by a Latin binomial e.g., **Homo sapiens**." That's us; we are different from plants, animals, and vegetation etc. The dictionary states that the scientific naming of species whereby each species receives a Latin or Latinized name of two parts. The first indicating the genus and the second being the specific epithet. For example: "Juglans regia is the English walnut; Juglans nigra, the black walnut /a kind or sort/ used humorously to refer to people who share a characteristic or occupation./ a particular kind of atom, molecule, ion, or particle./a group subordinate to a genus and containing individuals agreeing in some common attributes and called by a common name." All of this simply means that we are human beings: all races, colors, etc., and we all have the same basic DNA of **genes** and so forth which makes us all human beings.

Now that you and I have been "re-**gene** rated," we have

become a new race of beings that never before existed until God raised Jesus from the dead! We are now a new race, a super-human or supernatural race of beings that entered into the Kingdom of God only through the born-again experience. This was a mystery that was hid in God before the foundation of the world; a mystery that Satan had no knowledge of it; a mystery that changed everything forever (1 Corinthians 2:7-8; Colossians 1:26-27). Jesus (Yeshua) the Messiah is the head of this new species of being- born again man, the new man (Ephesians 1:22-23).

SEED PRODUCTION

St. John 12:24 states, "Verily, verily, I say unto you, Except a corn of wheat fall into the ground and die, it abideth alone; **but if it die,** it bringeth forth much fruit" (KJV). From the Amplified Bible, this verse states, "I assure you, most solemnly I tell you, Unless a grain of wheat falls into the earth and dies, it remains [just one grain; it never becomes more but lives] by itself alone, **But if it dies, it produces many others and yields a rich harvest.**" (Bold print added for emphasis)

This process of the growth of <u>a seed</u> into <u>a plant</u> is called germination. The life of a plant begins from a **tiny seed**. The seed is protected by an outer covering called a **seed coat**. The seed contains a small baby plant called an **embryo**.

There are certain <u>conditions required for the growth of a seed:</u>
   1. Moisture
   2. Warmth
   3. Nutrient rich soil
   4. Sunlight
   5. Good quality seed

<u>Once these conditions are satisfied, the seed begins its growth cycle or germination starts:</u>
- The seed absorbs water from the soil and provides moisture to the embryo.

- The plant cells inside the seed start duplicating.
- The Enzymes get activated.
- The Embryo starts getting nourishment.

The first sign of growth is a tiny root which comes out of the seed. With more and more nourishment, the embryo starts growing its time of photosynthesis. Eventually, the growing plant bursts open through the seed coat in search of sunlight **to start its own process of photosynthesis (plants prepare their own food with sunlight, carbon dioxide from air, and water from soil.** Once the seed coat falls off, the root starts growing downward to anchor the seed and to search for more food and nutrients from the soil. Meanwhile, the shoot also starts growing upward towards the light. Soon, we see a baby plant with tiny leaves.

Let us take a look at Hebrews 2:9-11. "9But we see Jesus, who was made a little lower than the angels, **for the suffering of death,** crowned with glory and honour; that he by the grace of God should **taste death for every man.** 10For it became him, for whom are all things, and by whom are all things, in bringing **many sons** unto glory, to make the captain of their salvation perfect through suffering. 11For both **he** that sanctifieth and **they** who are sanctified **are all of one:** for which cause he is not ashamed to call them brethren."

According to Ephesians 2:1, God through the death, burial, and resurrection of Jesus Christ took OUR **human spirit** that was dead unto him (God), and changed it into a new species of being by allowing us to die with Jesus on the cross and go down with Jesus into the region of hell and be totally transfigured into something new in order to redeem us back and change us into something that the devil will never be able to get a hold to again—not ever!

We are re-birth, new birth, born again, a superhuman race of beings with the life of God in us. Hallelujah! For when Jesus rose, we rose up with him! Christ Jesus is the grain of wheat that fell to the ground and <u>does not stand alone</u> for faith in His redeeming work produces sons (heirs) of God.

And if ye be Christ's, then are ye Abraham's seed, and heirs according to the promise (Galatians 3:29).

This new species, this new race of being are in Christ and heirs of God according to the promise. Hallelujah!

GOD AT WORK IN THE NEW SPECIES

Philippians 2:13 states, **"For it is God who worketh in you both to will and to work, for His good pleasure"** He is at work within you, solving your problems, building his strength into you, and making His wisdom your wisdom, His ability your ability, and His strength your strength.

This new species, new race of beings is "THE IMAGE OF GOD by Christ Jesus." You are the image of God through Christ Jesus. You are a new race, a species that never before existed. Let me explain to you what that means. By definition the word, **new creature,** means a person of a specified kind. Actually, it is talking about a new species of being, a new race of people among the normal or regular human beings. The regular human beings are those who have not been born again according to the Scripture; those who still have the nature of Satan in them which we all received from Adam after the fall of mankind. Ephesian 2:1 describes this condition as **"we were dead in trespass and sins."**

And the very God of peace sanctify you wholly; and I pray God your whole spirit and soul and body be preserved blameless unto the coming of our Lord Jesus Christ (I Thess. 5:23).

As a new species, we have to start looking at ourselves as a spirit being with a soul and living in a body. This will help us greatly in our walk with God as His image and as His sons and daughters. As we seek to operate our faith like Father God, in the name of Jesus, there will be divine increase in the power and operation of our faith's ability in God. Your spirit man is legal, born again with the very nature of God in it. Hallelujah!

FUNCTION LIKE GOD

You (the new species, the new race of being) have the ability to function like God because your inner man has the nature of God in it. I am teaching you about your human spirit, which we call the new species, so that you will know and understand that you can function like God legally. Everything created has the capability to operate according to its nature. The new species, the new race has God's nature, and it is His will that you operate your faith just like He does.

As a new species, I'm not depending upon my strength. I'm not doing this in my strength. I'm doing this in the strength my Father has given me according to who He says I am, what He says I am, what He says I can do, and how He has given me to operate in Him.

Now that's the proper management of that Scripture; that's the proper operation to those who are in Christ Jesus and are seated with Him in the heavenly places. That's the proper attitude of those who know who they are, who their God is, what they are, and how they are to operate in him. You know the tools and the keys that you are to use etc.

This is the manifestation of the Scripture: Let the weak say I am strong because you have submitted your weakness unto him and you are illustrating and demonstrating it by not depending upon your human strength which cannot accomplish the spiritual work of God.

His strength is made perfect in weakness, meaning you get out of yourself and depend upon him to work through you and get the job done through you. We do not operate in a God-like perspective or attitude when we read "his strength is made perfect in weakness." We have been taking on the wrong interpretation of it. We are to do what Colossians 3:10 says and *"put on the new man which is created after the image of him who created you."* This means to say, "Devil I come at you. Not in my name and not in my strength, but in the name of Jesus, by the authority that God has given me and the ability and power that He has given me to operate as His image and as His likeness in Jesus mighty name." Now go!

That's our attitude; that's our position. It is not an intimidated and fearful one, but as His image, as His likeness. Hallelujah! Now I see God patting you on your back saying, "That's my boy! That's my girl!"

Yes he (the devil) has power; yes he is the chief fallen angel of all the fallen angels and demons, but no angel is on the same level as the Father, the Son of God, which is the word of God, or the Holy Spirit (the Spirit of God and the Spirit of the Son in us). Neither is there any angel above the crown of God's creation: man.

Yes he (the devil) has power, but he does not have authority. You have authority in the earth realm and that authority was given to man by his creator Father God. It's time to be renewed in that knowledge, in that revelation, and understand it; embrace it and implement the Father's will in the earth realm. Why? Because the kingdom of God is here! It has made its arrival and we can enforce it in the spirit realm and in the natural. Whatever you're asking for or whatever you're looking for me to do, do not think that it is difficult for me to do or to give or get it to you! This is a vital key, a very important principle to operating your faith as a *son of God* and as a *little god* under your Father God in the earth realm.

- When I talk to you, position yourself like I showed you: think and say this is easy, this is so easy, this is so simple; act like it is easy, act like it is simple for me to do and for you to exercise your faith in me for it.
- Act and feel confident and sure about it (take on "this state of mind" every time) and refuse to move off of it or out of it!!!
- Act like it's happening right now, act like it's flowing right now! And it is so!
- Think like it, act like it, feel like it, praise and worship like it's happening right now, and it is so.

In doing and practicing these principles for a son of God and a *little god under Christ's rule*, you are keeping doubt, fear, and carnal thinking out of the way. This is a process of getting and keeping your carnal man out of the way, and this is the process and procedure of accepting and walking in the mind of Christ.

Let's take a look at faith in action. St. Matt. 14:28 states, **"and Peter answered him Lord, if it is you, command me to come to you on the water."** Jesus, giving a command to Peter, put him (Peter) on the same frequency you are on! If God has you out there, He's responsible! Peter, beginning to sink, had allowed doubt into his consciousness and accepted it and acted upon it! Yes, it is a Rhema word but look at this: Jesus is not the one who activated it or who initiated it; it was Peter. The Rhema word was in the form of and was asked for in the form of a command, and it was also a deep confirmation from Jesus to Peter that enabled him to move out and to step out of the boat.

Discovering who we are as the image of God will enable us to become masters over our situations, circumstances, conditions, challenges, and things we have to face, deal with, and conquer. We will first understand that we are a new species, a new race. In learning about it, seeing it, and being willing to implement it, we will learn that it is a core part of us exercising our ability to master our situations and circumstances. For being born of God gives you the ability and qualifies you to master situations and circumstances; to change them all; to stop them and even remove them. You are able to function like God because your spirit has been re-created like His Spirit. That's what the new species is: the new man created by God through Christ Jesus. Your inner man functions just like God. That's very important to know. You have to accept this biblical truth. If you do anything other than that, you will not be able to master your situations and circumstances in life like Jesus.

PRODUCTS OF THE RESURRECTION

And it was of His own [free] will that He gave us birth [as sons] by [His] word of truth, so that we should be a kind of firstfruits of His creatures [a sample of what He created to be consecrated to Himself] (James 1:18 Amplified).

The new man is a product of the resurrection of Christ. When Jesus achieved immortality of His flesh, that made Him the firstfruits and the believers the fruit to follow. This also means that God has accomplished the work first in our human spirit: the new species. As the new race of beings, we walk in a different mentality than regular human beings. We walk and operate in and through Christ and with the mind of Christ, which enables us to do extraordinary things as Christ releases the operation of supernatural ability in us and through us. Now we are the new man and we have a mindset that believes all things are possible with God and to him that believeth. We have accepted our identity and we will never be the same again!

For this is a set time to learn how to rule and reign with Christ in this life. And there is no turning back. The new man has the ability to exercise his will just

> *like his Father and Elder Brother in and through the Holy Spirit because your Father's will is your will and life. I seek not my will but my Father's, for we are one!*

Like your Father God, you are responsible for what you say; you're responsible for what you desire to be; you're responsible for how you use your authority and ability; you're responsible for how you use the name of Jesus as the image of God. This only works every time **you know who you are and operate in it** for God's glory! When you are quickened to act like God, when you see yourself acting like God, and quickened in Him to do so; when you believe that you will be quickened to act like God and step into it and do so, then you will show forth the true image of God.

This new race of beings, this new species, was created by God through Christ Jesus. That's why the Scriptures tell us that "as He is we shall be also" (I John 3:1-2). It is not yet manifested what we shall be like except that we shall have bodies like His glorified human body. This will be at the rapture (Phil.3:20-21; I Cor. 15:51-54; Col. 3:4). Every person will have his own body, color, features, and characteristics, as on earth (I Cor. 15:35-54).

This new creature, this new creation which God created through Christ Jesus, is a duplication of what Jesus became when God raised him from the dead. Romans 8:29 states, **"For whom he did foreknow he also did predestinate to be conformed to the image of his Son, that he might be the firstborn among many brethren."** In this verse, and in other New Testament passages, the word, "firstborn," is the Greek word, *prototokos* (Rom. 8:29; Col. 1:15-18; Heb. 1:6; 11:28; 12:23; Rev. 1:5).

First Corinthians 15:20 states, **"But now is Christ risen from the dead and become the first fruits of them that slept."** Christ's resurrection is an eternal fact and the guarantee of the resurrection of all other men. In this verse, the Greek word, *aparche*, is used for the English word, first fruits, and it means *the beginning of a thing.* This means that Christ is the first to be resurrected from the dead and enter into immortality of the body (v51-54). By Adam came physical death, which is a result of the eternal death penalty of sin (see 1 Cor. 15:22). This death passed upon all men (Rom 5:12-21). The body only will be resurrected in the future resurrection of the dead (1 Cor. 15:35-54; Dan. 12:2; Jn. 5:28-29), which is the only time spiritual and eternal deaths can be canceled. Resurrecting one from being dead in trespasses and sin is in this earthly life (Eph. 2:1-9; I Jn. 1:9). After physical death, comes the judgment without any chance to be saved, if one dies unsaved (Heb. 9:27).

NO LONGER COMMON

You can understand now that you are not common anymore. You belong to an unusual order of beings. You are a New Creation created in Christ Jesus (Ephesians 2:10), and you are created to an end: to enter into a certain realm, to do His will, and carry out His purposes here on earth. You have a testimony now that is thrilling. You remember that your faith will keep track with your testimony. Your faith and confession must match, because if it doesn't, you cannot receive because they are connected. You will never have faith beyond what you confess for there is a relation between your faith and your confession.

If you are afraid to confess your oneness with Him—His life is your life, His ability is your ability, His wisdom is your wisdom, and His strength is your strength—if you are afraid to confess it, it is not yours. It is what you boldly say before the enemy that fills him with fear and paralyzes him, yet fills you with power, courage, and victory that it is yours in reality. If you are halting and have a negative confession, your faith will never rise above it.

A negative confession shows a lack of respect and appreciation on your part in regards to Christ's victory over Satan. You are identified with Christ. When He conquered Satan, before He arose from the dead, you were with Him in that combat through the law of identification, and the victory that He achieved is laid to your account. All you have to do is to take your place and say, "Satan in the name of Jesus Christ of Nazareth, leave me now" or you say, "Leave that loved one right now!" When you quote Jesus' word, it is exactly as if He were speaking it himself. You remember Jesus said, **"The words that I speak they are not Mine, but they are my Father's."** So, when Jesus commanded diseases to leave those bodies, it was his Father speaking. So, when you order disease to leave bodies in Jesus' name, it is as though your Father were speaking. You can't confess negativity and operate in power and authority. When you have a negative testimony and you talk about your lack, shortages, and your weakness, the adversary takes advantage of your confession with what you are saying out of your mouth and brings you down to the level of it. But we don't want to operate like that!

We need to pray from the knowledge of who we are in Christ and stay focused. Utilize all your spiritual weapons, especially praying in tongues.

He that speaketh in an unknown tongue speaketh not unto men but unto God. (I Cor. 14:2)

Therefore, when I pray, I focus on the truth that I am a new species of being and I begin to speak in tongues focusing on the fact that I am a new species—I am the new man. I address the Father in tongues or when I am praying in tongues, I focus on my belly—the core of my recreated human spirit—and I am accessing God in me for directions, clearing, clarity, strengthening, and confirmation etc. I am listening directly to God in my inner man, the new species, who has the nature of God in it. I know that it is accurate and sure because in tongues, I have a direct line of communication with God! What He speaks in me, He also confirms in me and quickens His word from His word within me.

Now this sets the new creation, the new species, above and beyond regular human beings. God's life and light are in me! Hallelujah! We are superior; we are more than conquerors etc.

A SUPERIOR RACE OF BEINGS

As children of God, we are like God. We want to understand the new God-like nature in us and how to look to it and operate from it. Let's first understand that because we have the nature of God in this human body we are like God. This isn't something that we came up with ourselves. It is what God himself has done in us through Jesus Christ. My job is to help you discover who you are by showing you your true identity which brings you revelation of what you can do and how you can operate as the image of God because your **inner-man** is created just like him: like Jesus. In doing this, you will change your thinking to match what God has already done in you.

The life of God, the Spirit of God, and the nature of God are sufficient for every need of man. – *For there is a realm where things happen supernaturally for you – you said whatever we ask in your name you would give it to us. Right now we operate within the level of faith that we have been taught whether from our family or denominational teaching, etc. Power to do is available to all who would dare walk in it. The thing is to believe that what you say will come to pass and to see it happening. The prophet of God said in 2 Kings "…tomorrow about this time wheat will be sold for a shekel in the gates of Samaria." And it happened. That's a glimpse of the new species. There are places that we are afraid to walk in or we think that they are not for us to walk. We must grow in the understanding and knowledge that we can change things- we must also believe that we can know things about what is- "right now" and about what will happen- e.g. we can know what will happen with our bills or government- anything and everything that we may face. IF YOU MOVE YOURSELF THEN GOD CAN HAVE HIS WAY!*

We are the superior race: the new species. We are a superior race of beings that is not like the devastatingly, colossal, historical murders, and genocides that have plagued the human race. We have had such demonically warped minds thinking that their race is superior to others based upon skin color, their eye color, abilities, the country they are from, etc. From the Germans with the Nazis who sought to create a society based entirely on warped concepts of racial and biological "purity" (bbc.co.uk website the Nazi racial state by Prof. Peter Longerich, last update 2011-02-17), to the Russians with white supremacy that all other races are beneath them, etc. This is another demonic principle from the fall of Adam. Dr. Martin Luther King, Jr. said, "For black supremacy is just as bad as white supremacy. It is through salvation and education that changes a man's heart. This puts us all on the even playing field"

Jesus said, "I know what is in man," and He also said, "Why callest thou me good? There is none good but one, that is, God." There are others trying to make or grow the perfect man in the laboratories etc. The Adonis! Like the Greeks of Old, they are making gods and goddesses, etc., and destroying lesser so-called races and groups of people. However, the real and true superior race or superior human beings is **the new species**. It is the born-again believers who have decided to take their place in oneness with God as his sons and daughters who recognize and understand that they are something new! Our superiority is not something in and of ourselves but it is by God, from God, and through God unto us because of Our Lord and Savior Jesus Christ. Our superiority is never designed to "steal, kill, and destroy," but it is designed for life and that more abundantly. We show forth the glory of God in knowledge, revelation, relationship, and the fulfillment of purpose in the earth realm.

OPERATING FAITH FROM A DIFFERENT POSITION

In describing the "New Species," it's not just talking about faith: how we believe, how we set our faith, or how we operate our faith. Being a new species explains why we operate our faith the way we do. As a new species, we operate our faith from a different positioning and that positioning is like God and/or a son of God, which means we believe that what we say will come to pass and that what we say is accomplishing things in the unseen realm of the spirit, it will not return to us void.

Most of us quote Isaiah 55:11 only in relations to God and Jesus and we exclude ourselves from it. However, this realm of identity belongs to us. We are a part of the Godhead family stationed here on earth. It is our inheritance also, but we have not been enforcing it because we lacked the reality and revelation knowledge of what we are: "a new species of being," a supernatural race of beings.

To keep this dimension strong and vibrant, we have to keep our minds renewed to it by:

   A. Maintaining fellowship with God
   B. Maintaining obedience to the Holy Spirit
   C. Constant meditation upon this word (you are the

image of God)
  D. Keeping a confession of faith with it

Accepting who you are as the image of God changes your image and view of yourself; changes your image and view of the devil and how you deal with him; changes your image and view of how you exercise your faith; changes your image and view of your relationship with God; changes your image and view of the Holy Spirit. You will have more control over yourself, more control over your environment, and more control over the enemy. Areas and dimensions of faith that you shy away from or that you were afraid to enter into, or to operate in, you will move into them now. Demonic strongholds and demonic powers that you refused to address, or that you were afraid to address in the past, you will be able to address them—or it. This same thing goes with your family, etc.

The New Species thinks differently. A new species thinks differently than regular human beings. That's right! Their thinking, their attitude, and the way they process information spiritually is different than regular human beings. They have a different mindset! They have (1) a God-like mindset, (2) a Kingdom mindset, (3) a son of God mindset, and this mindset is directed toward every area and operation of their lives. They do not evaluate things like regular people do because their minds are always subject to the Holy Spirit and the biblical principles of the word of God. They evaluate things from and by revelation from the Spirit of God their Father. In other words, they evaluate things and events from God's opinion and God's point-of-view just like Jesus Christ of Nazareth did! Jesus stated, "I do always those things which please my Father." Likewise, we hear from the Father, we ask him; He reveals things to us by our new spirit man and the Holy Ghost.

The new species has a normal life, but it is governed by and in subjection to the authority of the Kingdom of God. Any time they fall short, they get right back up in that realm! The new species is both man and god or should I say both human and divine (deity).

It requires a recreated spirit to grasp the things of the Spirit of God, for they are foolishness to the un- re-**gene**rated man (I Cor. 2:14). It requires a recreated spirit to grasp the things of God whether those things are in the mental, physical, or spiritual realm.

Do not operate in fear—fear not for the Scripture says, **"For God did not give us a spirit of timidity (of cowardice, of craven and cringing and fawning fear), but (He has given us a spirit) of power and love and of calm, and well-balanced mind and discipline and self-control" (2 Tim. 1:7 Amplified.** Fear is not just a spirit; it is also **a choice.** You have a decision to make whether to accept it and operate in it or to ignore it and step forward in spite of it! Unbelief is a spirit but it is also **a choice**-- you can choose not to believe or you can choose to believe. Thomas said, "I will not believe until I see the nail print in his hands…" Jesus said, "Blessed are they that believe and have not seen, and yet have believed" (St. John 20:29).

God wants us to look to our new nature within us. That's why the word of God contains statements such as: "Greater is he that's in you," and "You have been born of God." You overcome the world because of what you are, what God has made you. Therefore, when you don't know who you are, what you are, and what you can do, it's obvious you won't utilize them. If you haven't been taught to look to the nature of God which is in you, how can you get the results that God wants us to have from it and because of it?

He keeps talking about the results of what happens when a person is born of God (pointing toward your **inner man**, the **new man** who is born of God and has the nature of God in it). That nature affects his character, personality, and his conversation. It affects his response to things in the world and it affects his faith. Knowing that you have the nature of God in you indicates that you are like God and should operate like Him. We must learn to look to the nature within us for the kingdom of God is within you, if you have been born-again. God's new work has been wrought in you: the Word made manifest = you have received a new nature from God through Christ Jesus.

The new birth, the results of the Kingdom of heaven inhabiting earthen vessels, the regeneration process that happened in you, is from above and not from the earth realm. Therefore, you have been birthed into the Kingdom of God. The Kingdom of God is within you, not just the Holy Spirit being in you, but also what you are through the new birth. You are a new species of being called **inner man**, **new man**, which is your human spirit. It now has the nature of God in it for it was that nature that changed it (you). We call it eternal life- the Kingdom of God, the life of God is in your nature. As a matter of fact, that is your new nature for the old nature passed out of you when you were born again by the power of God.

The Scripture states, "To as many as received him gave he them power to become sons of God (John 1:12). The Scripture also says in First John chapter five, "4For whatsoever is born of God overcometh the world: and this **IS** the victory that overcometh the world even our faith. 5Who is he that overcometh the world, but he that believeth that Jesus is the Son of God?"

Let's also take a look at two more verses in that chapter:

"12He that hath the Son **hath life**; and he that hath not the Son of God hath **not life.** 13These things have I written unto you that believe on the name of the Son of God; that ye may know that ye **have eternal life**, and that ye may believe on the name of the Son of God" (bold print added for emphasis) .

THE ZOE LIFE OF GOD

Possessing the nature of God means that eternal life is yours now. The life of God is in you, you have **the Zoe life of God** in you right now, not when you die and go to heaven, but right now! Let's take a look at an excerpt from Dr. Long's book, *Walking in Truth*.

> *"For too many Believers, eternal life is futuristic, something to be experienced when they get to heaven. For that cause, they do nothing to develop a right now fellowship with Jesus. They do not seek to know Jesus in an intimate way but are satisfied with the worship of a God who is mysterious in nature and who they will understand "better by and by" or in other words, when they get to heaven. Because these Believers continue to walk in the carnality of the soul, without divine purpose, and without the understanding or guidance of the Holy Spirit, they feel that whatever they fair in life is their appointed lot. These Believers fail to understand that the Spirit of Life imparted eternal life at the new birth experience, not for ornamental purposes, but that it might be experienced here on the earth as the doorway into divine purpose and victorious living. These Believers fail to understand that eternal life has to do with receiving the nature of God into the human spirit, and not just confessing belief in Jesus to secure a place in heaven.*

> *Those who are born–again have the very nature of Christ residing on the inside of their human spirit—they have Zoe-life (p. 271).*

There are four different Greek words translated *life* in the New Testament:
  a. Zoe meaning the God-kind of life
  b. Psuche meaning human life
  c. Bios meaning manner of life
  d. Anastrophe meaning confused behavior

In the Greek, the word for the God-kind of LIFE is *Zoe*. The English phrases that we are accustomed to are *eternal life* and *everlasting* life. The term eternal life is the root to our conversation and revelation of what God has both called us and made us.

THE MIRACLE THAT HAPPENED TO OUR HUMAN SPIRIT MADE US A NEW SPECIES. That miracle is called the new birth: the impartation of Zoe life into our spirit recreating it into the image of God. It is the new nature that delivered us from spiritual death and placed us in the Kingdom of God.

WHAT IS DEATH?

The Bible speaks of two types of deaths: physical and spiritual. According to Wikipedia, death (physical) is "the permanent cessation of all biological functions that sustain a living organism. Phenomena which commonly bring about death include aging, predation, malnutrition, disease, suicide, homicide, starvation, dehydration, and accidents or major trauma resulting in terminal injury. In most cases, bodies of living organisms begin to decompose shortly after death." (Wikipedia. org)

Most people have the wrong view of what death is because of our attachment to life, living, affections, companionship, and our loved ones, etc. Death (physical) doesn't mean annihilation but separation from the physical body. In Genesis 3:19, God informed Adam, *"In the sweat of thy face shalt thou eat bread, till thou return unto the ground; for out of it wast thou taken: for dust thou art, and unto dust shalt thou return."* It is because of sin that man's physical body dies and goes back to the dust! However, the person inside of the body lives on because they are made like unto God: spirit beings.

Now let's give you the Bible definition of death. The word, *death*, as applied to man in Scripture, means separation, or a cutting off from realizing God's purpose for which he was created. Physical death is the separation of the inner man from the outer man; the soul and spirit from the body.

St. James 2:26 states that "For as the body without the spirit is dead, so faith without works is dead also." Only the body dies at the time of physical death. This is caused by the soul and spirit leaving the body. The body returns to dust and the soul and spirit of the righteous go to heaven to await the resurrection (2 Cor. 5:8; Phil. 1:21-24; Heb. 12:23; Rev. 6:9-11). However, the soul and spirit of the wicked go to hell to await the final resurrection (Lk. 16: 19-31; Isa. 14:9; Rev. 20:11-15). **The soul and spirit are spiritual and immortal. They cannot go back to dust.**

Second Corinthians 5:17 states, *"Therefore if any man be in Christ he is a new creature old things are passed away and behold all things are become new."* He is a new creature means a new creation, a new species of being; a race of human beings that never before existed until Jesus (Yeshua) was raised from the dead. We are a duplication of what Christ is on the inside of that body. We have received a new nature, which means that our human spirit has been changed—metamorphosed—regenerated into a being that has never before existed. Called the new man, inward man, a new life, being born again means that our human spirit has been changed like unto His spirit: we have his nature.

The nature of God in us isn't a separate nature, a different nature from His in us—NO! When God regenerated us through repentance and acceptance of Jesus as Lord and Savior, we were actually born of the incorruptible seed, the word of God, which liveth and abideth for- ever. Jesus had to do his total transfiguration thing down here to make us God's seed—born again in our spirit. That word of God **caused a miracle to happen in our human spirit which is who we are: we are a spirit with a soul and we live in a body physically (your human spirit is who you are and what you are—not I have the nature of God in me and that**

nature is separate from my nature—no! I have only one nature and that is God's nature= God likeness).

My human spirit is like God's now. It is actually a duplication of Jesus spirit—the spirit of the man called Jesus Christ. Being God, He had the nature of God in Him and then he received sin into His spirit on the cross and He died, gave up the ghost; He went down into hell, but the story doesn't stop there. Praise God, the word of the Lord came to Him in hell just like it did on the surface of the earth when He obeyed Scripture and was baptized by His cousin John the Baptist. At that baptism, the Holy Ghost descended upon Him (Jesus) like a dove and the Father spoke from heaven saying, ***"This is my beloved son in whom I am well pleased; hear ye him."*** When the Father spoke like that about Him, it made Jesus the final authority in the earth realm, and that word was preserved for Him in the Psalms, the Law, and the prophets before He made it here in the physical realm. The Scripture is full of prophetic decrees telling the suffering Jesus would endure before dying on the cross; things that would take place in the grave, and His resurrection from death (Heb. 1:5, 6; Ps. 2:6, 7; Ps. 22). HE DID THIS TO MAKE US A NEW RACE OF BEINGS (A NEW SPECIES) THAT WILL NEVER DIE, MADE LIKE HIM, AND HAVING THE SAME NATURE AS HIS IN US!

Now when Jesus obeyed the Father and willingly died on the cross and said to the Father **"into thy hands I commit my spirit,"** that's like saying, "Father, I'm going all the way and I am trusting in you now as I go to the lower parts of the earth into Sheol." Here you see Jesus still operating from the Scriptures about Himself; each step, all the way, and when Jesus made the statement, ***"My God My God why has thou forsaken me,*** this had to happen because Jesus had to receive sin into His spirit and the Father had to separate from Him for a moment in order for Jesus to take the same penalty and punishment that Adam did in the beginning (sin came into Adam's spirit through disobedience and God said that he would die because of it). Jesus knew that this part had to take place. This is why he was praying in the garden and asking if there was another way. Jesus did not want to be separated from His Father for that time! Here is where faith comes in (the leaning of the whole personality on God and trusting in his goodness). The Father couldn't look at Jesus and fellowship with Him then. But, of course, Jesus didn't doubt His Father's love or His promise. Let's take a fresh look at the Scriptures pertaining to the crucifixion:

> *Jesus cried with a loud voice, saying Eloi, Eloi, lama sabachthani? Which is being interpreted, My God, My God, why hast thou forsaken me? (St. Mark 15:33-38; Ps. 22:1; Matt. 27:46)*

> *And about the ninth hour Jesus cried with a loud voice, saying, Eli, Eli, lama sabachthani? That is to say, My God, my God, why hast thou forsaken me? (St. Matt. 27:45-51; Heb. 5:7; Ps. 22:1)*

> *And straightway one of them ran, and took a sponge, and filled it with vinegar, and put it on a reed, and gave him to drink. (St. Matt. 27:48; Ps. 69:21; Mark 15:36)*

> *The rest said, Let be, let us see whether Elias will come to save him. Jesus, when he had cried again with a loud voice, yielded up the ghost (St. Matt. 27:49-50; Mark 13:37; Luke 23:46)*

> *And behold, the veil of the temple was rent in twain from the top to the bottom; and the earth did quake, and the rocks rent; (St. Matt. 27:51; Ex. 26:31; 2 Chr. 3:14)*

God had Scriptures prepared for Jesus before He went to paradise and into hell itself—into Satan's domain. Jesus did all this by faith for He said, *"I have power to lay it down, and I have power to take it again. This commandment have I received of my Father" (St. John 10:18b).* I tell you again that Jesus had to do all of this by faith for he said, *"Father, into your hands I commit my spirit"* knowing that where he went by faith that the word of God and the Spirit of God would be there.

When Jesus went to hell, He satisfied justice and judgment, and created great grace and mercy for us through the sacrifice of Himself. He satisfied the courts, God's wrath, and purchased grace, mercy, and new life for all humanity (Rev.21:5): those who would accept His love sacrifice of Himself for us to bring us back to the Father through making a new covenant with Jesus in our behalf.

HE CARRIED THE TRANSGRESSION (SIN) OF ADAM IN HIS SPIRIT DOWN INTO HELL ITSELF. HOW WAS HE ABLE TO DO THAT? BECAUSE HE IS GOD! AND MAN! - HE IS THE ONLY PERSON WHO COULD DO SUCH A THING. HE WAS BROUGHT INTO THE WORLD TO DO SUCH A THING. NO OTHER PERSON, NO HUMAN BEING COULD ACCOMPLISH SUCH A FEAT! HE WAS BORN BOTH TO DIE AND TO ARISE FROM THE DEAD AS SOMETHING NEW—A RESURRECTED GOD-MAN!!!! IN ST. JOHN 12:27, JESUS STATED, *"BUT FOR THIS CAUSE CAME I UNTO THIS HOUR,"* FOR REMEMBER HE IS STILL BOTH RIGHT NOW! OH! HALLELUJAH! HE BECAME THE AUTHOR OF ETERNAL SALVATION UNTO ALL

THEM THAT OBEY HIM AND HE WAS CALLED OF GOD TO THE NEW OFFICE –AN OFFICE THAT GOD CREATED HIMSELF ABOVE THE OFFICE OF THE AARONIC-LEVITICAL PRIESTHOOD—THE OFFICE OF A GREAT HIGH PRIEST AFTER THE ORDER OF MELCHISEDEC (Heb. 5:8-10).

Even after a temporary manifestation of transfiguration on the mountain with Peter, James, and John, when Moses and Elijah appeared unto him in a vision--even after what they said to Him to encourage Him and strengthen Him. Moses and Elijah said, "You will go to Jerusalem," "you will die," "God will raise you up!" (St. Matt. 17:1-13; Mark. 9:2-10; St. Luke 9:28-36). Even after that, Satan still did not understand the fullness of what God the Father had planned for us! (1 Cor. 2:6-9) Look at verse 8: **"Which none of the princes of this world knew: for had they known it, they would not have crucified the Lord of glory"** (see also Matt. 11:25; Luke 23:34).

So, he (the devil) went ahead and had Jesus killed and thought he would be able to keep Him in hell like the other godly men and women who were waiting on the promise of God. He (Satan) didn't know that God had prophecy promises prepared for Jesus hidden in the Psalms, the Law of Moses, and in the prophets for when He would be down in hell (St. Luke 24:44).

At the same time of praising God, Jesus' complete transfiguration took place. His form was changed. They had never seen anything like it before. The only begotten Son of God was transformed into something so great, so profound, which was hidden all the time in the mind of God. It destroyed all the power of Satan over mankind for Jesus took the keys of death, hell, and the grave (Rev.1:17-18). Look at the testimony of Jesus in verse 18: *"I am he that liveth, and was dead, and behold, I am alive for evermore,*

Amen: and have the keys of hell and of death" (see also Rom. 4:9; 6:9; Ps. 68:20).

THE WORD (JESUS) IS TOTALLY GOD- MAN NOW AND THAT GOD-MAN (JESUS), AFTER PREACHING AND LEADING CAPTIVITY CAPTIVE, HE STEPPED BACK INTO THE FLESH HOUSE, CAME OUT OF THAT TOMB, LAID THE GARMENT TO THE SIDE FOLDED; AND WHEN MARY CAME TO THE TOMB, HE (JESUS) APPEARED UNTO HER IN HIS RESURRECTED BODY THAT CAN BE HANDLED AND DEALT WITH—THAT CAN BREATHE, EAT, AND DRINK!

So Jesus went to hell by faith in His Father's promise to Him, and when he got there, the devil thought they had Jesus and that they were eternally successful, but the word of God came to Jesus in hell by the power of the Holy Spirit saying, *"I will not leave you in hell neither suffer my Holy One to see, corruption" (Ps. 16:10 paraphrased). "I will declare the decree: the LORD hath said unto me, Thou are my Son; this day have I begotten thee" (Ps. 2:7).*

These Scriptures had to be fulfilled about Jesus and only when He went to hell itself. Again, Psalm 16:10 states, *"For thou wilt not leave my soul in hell; neither wilt thou suffer thine Holy One to see corruption"* (underscoring added). We also see prophecy in Psalm 49:15, which states, *"But God will redeem my soul from the power of the grave: for he shall receive me. [Selah]"*

Just like Jesus had to fulfill the Scripture that declared they cast lots for his garment (Psalms 22:18), each of these seemingly isolated Scriptures or prophetic words spoken about the birth, life, death, and resurrection of our Lord Jesus Christ had to be fulfilled too. Here are some of the Scriptures that had to be fulfilled only when He (Jesus) was in hell itself:

- *Many bulls have compassed me: strong bulls of Bashan*

have beset me round (Ps. 22:12).
- *I will declare thy name unto my brethren: in the midst of the congregation will I praise thee (Ps. 22:22).*
- *Whither shall I go from thy spirit? or whither shall I flee from thy presence? If I ascend up into heaven, thou art there: if I make my bed I hell, behold, thou art there: if I make my bed in hell, behold, thou art there. If I take the wings of the morning, and dwell in the uttermost parts of the sea; Even there shall thy hand lead me, and thy right hand shall hold me (Ps. 139:7-10).*

Jesus became something new right down there before them in Hell and paradise. Then He said, *"I will praise your name in the midst of the great congregation,"* so He praised God His Father right before them. God had to say that Scripture to Him while he was in hell because the word says, *"I will not leave his soul in hell neither will I allow my Holy One to see corruption!" (Ps. 16:10 paraphrased)*. So, God spoke those words *"I will declare a decree... Thou art my son this day have I begotten thee (Ps. 2:7). "I will declare the decree..."* meaning He spoke down in hell and loosened Jesus from the demons and Jesus praised God while He was down there and unleashed the power of the Holy Ghost in that place (Rom. 1:4).

Jesus manifested in total transfiguration or total transformation of His spirit man right there in hell before them, and they could not contain it or Him, and that's when and how he took the keys from Satan (through the glory that was released down there). Jesus' total new resurrected being was received by an authority far above Satan's power. Anything that Satan could think he would want to do to Jesus or with Him, He couldn't! Jesus' body could not see corruption, for the Scripture declared "*.... nor suffer my*

Holy One to see corruption," which refers to the body only.

Jesus had told them already before it happened that he is the resurrection and the life and he paid the price for the fullness of it—a total resurrected being. He is the first-fruit to arise from the dead, and He got back into that physical body raised by the Holy Spirit. Now we see how dependent He was upon the Holy Spirit. As prophetically uttered by David in the psalms, *"...no matter where you are, my Spirit will be there (paraphrased)."*

From Hebrews 2:9, we see evidence that Jesus received sin into his spirit while on the cross (see also Gal. 3:13). Because the Scripture declares in Isaiah 53:10-11 and Hebrews 2:9 *"But we see Jesus, who was made a little lower than the angels, for the suffering of death, crowned with glory and honor; that he by the grace of God SHOULD TASTE DEATH FOR EVERY MAN" (see also verses 10-18).* Look at how Jesus used His faith trusting in His Father and following the leadership of the Holy Spirit. Jesus was completely submissive to the Holy Spirit even during the time of making Himself our offering for sin. Jesus believed that the Father, by the Holy Spirit, would raise Him up again.

We have the example of Abraham offering up his only promised son Isaac to whom the promises were made (Gen. 22:10-14). Abraham had to walk in it (the offering up of Isaac) first before God could bring in Jesus to walk in it (the offering of self) in reality. Now Jesus walked in Sonship so that we could walk in sonship. So, what you see Jesus operating in before the resurrection is a glimpse of our place of sonship—sons of God (those who make it to this realm of maturity and anointing). Hallelujah!) WE ARE A NEW SPECIES OF BEING NOT OF THIS WORLD BUT OF THE WORLD TO COME! We are manifesting now in the earth realm to complete and fulfill all of the will of God as Jesus is making preparation to return and catch us away. We are taking dominion, ruling and reigning with Christ in this life, and placing every enemy under His feet! Hallelujah x3!

As a new species of being, we dwell in Christ and Christ dwells in us. That same level of faith and power Jesus operated in while here on earth is available to the new species of being. The fullness of God that is in Christ Jesus is also in us through the presence of the Holy Spirit dwelling on the inside of us. Wow! Now that's a powerful statement. The fullness is in Him (Jesus) and He (Jesus) lives in us. The Bible confirms this statement in several places:

   1. **All of Jesus is in us**: 1 John 4:4; Eph. 2:21, 4:13; Col. 1:19, 2:9-10, 19; St. John 1:16

   2. **His fullness in us:** Eph. 1:23, 3:19; Gal. 2:20

   3. **He is in us:** St. John chapter 15, 17:21-24; 1 John 4:12, 17

All that Jesus accomplished on the cross, He did to make us a NEW RACE OF BEINGS (A NEW SPECIES) THAT WILL NEVER DIE. Jesus did it so that we could be made like Him, having the same nature as He. Hallelujah!

NEW SPECIES DAILY CONFESSION

I am the Image of God. I am created in God's image and in God's likeness. I have the nature of God in me and that nature of God is the life of God. Because I have God's nature in me, I can act just like Him, I can speak just like Him, and I can believe just like Him.

Therefore, I look to that new nature and not to my old self, old mind, or old nature because old things have passed away (II Cor. 5:17). The Nature of God is in me and I look to God's presence in me.

Nature of God, you are the light of me that means the development of me. I've got the nature of God, the light of God in me and I must walk in it in order for it to benefit me. Therefore sickness, disease, lack, poverty, and shortage-- these have no place in me. I now confess that the life of God is in me!

I have God's wisdom in me. I have God's life in me. I have God's power in me. I have God's ability in me. The nature of God is in me! Therefore, because of this, I'm in union with God and my spirit, soul, and body reject all sickness, disease, lack, poverty, and shortage. They may come by my way, BUT THEY CANNOT LAST, CANNOT STICK because the nature of God doesn't consist of any of these things. They cannot stay because they are not the nature of God, and the nature of God doesn't receive them. Therefore, I do not have them nor walk in them.

Again, I say my body, soul, spirit, and appetite reject sickness, demons, poverty, ignorance, lack of money, and shortage because I have the nature of God in me. That nature is wisdom, health, wealth, life—and that more abundantly. That nature, God's nature in me, is knowledge, good success, and good intellect, plus much more.

I am in union with God; therefore, there should not be any failure in me unless I willed my time away not knowing what I've got, or not confessing it, and not acting upon it. I say this life is mine; praise God it's in me and it's working thank God.

As the Image of God, I can operate in dominion principles. Therefore, being one with God as a New Species, I take dominion. I have "dominion and authority through Christ." I take dominion. As the Image of God in Christ Jesus, I bring things into order and subjection to the kingdom of God. I take back the DOMINION which was lost in the Garden of Eden. For it is time for me to "rule and reign with Christ in this life".

THEREFORE, I SAY, "I AM BLESSED AND HIGHLY FAVORED. I HAVE FAVOR WITH GOD AND WITH MAN. WHATEVER I SET MY HANDS TO DO DOES PROSPER. BUSINESSES, PEOPLE, PLACES AND THINGS PROSPER BECAUSE I AM THE BLESSED OF THE LORD. MONEY LOVES ME; MONEY COMES TO ME! BECAUSE I AM THE IMAGE OF GOD, I AM COVERED IN THE BLOOD OF JESUS! THE ANGELS OF GOD HAVE CHARGE OVER ME!" THEREFORE, I SAY, "NO WEAPON FORMED AGAINST ME SHALL PROPER."

BIBLIOGRAPHY

Holy Bible: King James Version. Thomas Nelson Publisher.
Nashville, Tennessee, 1989.

Holy Bible: The Everyday Life Bible Amplified Version.
Warner Faith. New York, New York, 2006 by Joyce Meyer.

Long, Ednorleatha. *Walking In Truth*. Good News Publications. East St. Louis, Illinois, 2009.

Strong, James. Strong's Exhaustive Concordance of the Bible.
Hendrickson Publishers. Peabody, Massachusetts.

Webster's Collegiate Dictionary. World Publishing Company.
Cleveland and New York, 1960.

Made in the USA
Monee, IL
13 September 2021